Stories from
The Bible
for Children

Brown Watson
ENGLAND

Index

Old Testament

New Testament

God Creates
Heaven and Earth

*L*ong, long ago there was nothing at all, only darkness. Then God said, 'Let there be light!' And so, there was light, shining into the darkness. That was the end of the first day of God's creation.

*N*ext day, God carried on with his work, creating the heavens and the Earth. 'Let there be a sky!' he said. And so, there was a blue sky, high above the Earth. Then, it was the end of the second day. But, seas still covered the Earth. So, on the third day, God made dry land appear. Here, trees and plants and flowers and grasses grew. Then on the fourth day, God made the sun to shine in the sky by day and the moon and the stars to shine at night-time. On the fifth day, God made birds to fly in the sky and fish and animals to live in the seas.

On the sixth day, God made all kinds of animals to live on the Earth. He made a man and called him Adam. On the seventh day, God rested. He trusted Adam to look after all living things on Earth. Then God made a beautiful garden for Adam to live in. It was called The Garden of Eden. Whilst Adam slept, God created a woman. Adam would call her Eve.

*I*n the middle of The Garden of Eden stood a special tree. This was the Tree of Knowledge of Good and Evil. 'You can eat the fruit from any tree in the garden,' God had told Adam, 'except from the Tree of Knowledge. If you do, you will die.' Adam had never eaten the fruit. But, one day, a snake slithered down from the tree, ready to tempt Eve. 'Why not taste the fruit of this tree?' it hissed at her. 'Then you will be as wise as God.'

$\mathcal{E}$ve picked a fruit from the Tree of Knowledge. How delicious it tasted! She picked another and gave it to Adam. But, instead of being happy, now they felt sad and ashamed, because they had no clothes. They covered themselves with leaves from the fig tree.

God saw that Adam and Eve had disobeyed him by eating the fruit from the Tree of Knowledge. They could no longer be trusted and so they had to leave the Garden of Eden. God sent down an angel to see that they could never return. Now, Adam would have to work the land to grow his own food.

$\mathcal{A}$dam knew he could not work the land on his own. He was glad when he and Eve had two sons, Cain and Abel.

Cain was the elder brother.
He farmed the land and
Abel looked after the sheep.

*I*n time, Cain made an offering to God of the first fruits of his work in the fields. Abel offered one of the first lambs from his flock. God was more pleased with the lamb, because he knew Abel had given it with all his heart. This made Cain very angry.

Cain was jealous of Abel. One day, as they were out walking, he hurled himself down on his brother and killed him. God saw what Cain had done and made him leave the land, never to return.
God comforted Adam and Eve by giving them another son, called Seth. And, from this son, all the people on Earth would be descended.

Noah
and his Family

*H*undreds of years passed. More people lived on
God's Earth. But, all was not well. There was so
much wickedness, God felt sad that he had created
human beings at all. He looked around to find one
good man. His name was Noah.

God told Noah, 'I must destroy everything that is bad in the world, otherwise, the world will be spoilt by evil and wickedness. To do this, I shall send a great flood. But you, Noah, will be saved. I want you to build an ark of strong wood for yourself and your family, big enough to take two of every kind of animal!' Noah did all that God asked him.

$\mathcal{N}$ot long after the ark was
finished and all the animals were on board,
it began to rain. For forty days and forty nights
it rained without stopping. The ark stayed afloat.

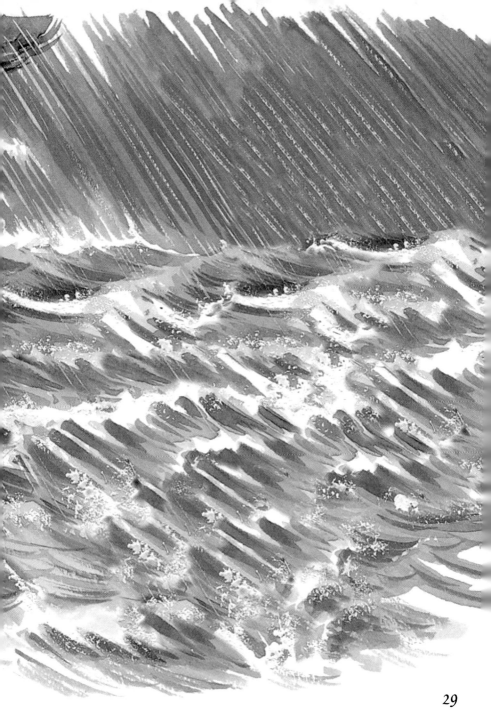

*T*he waters
covered the highest mountains.
Every living thing on Earth perished
- plants, animals and people.

Then God sent warm winds which began to dry up the waters. Noah sent out a raven but it did not return. Then he sent out a dove. At first, the dove came back. Noah tried again and the dove returned with a leaf in its beak. So Noah knew the flood levels were going down. Soon, he was able to bring the ark safely to dry land. All the animals were able to leave the ark.

God told Noah, 'You may leave the ark, too. I will never again send such a flood to destroy the Earth. Look up to the clouds and see the sign that I will keep my promise.' Noah and his family looked up to the sky. They saw a beautiful rainbow.

*T*he descendants of Noah and his family spread out towards all parts of the Earth. When they came to a place called Shinar, they thought it was so beautiful that they decided to settle there. They began to make bricks to build a city.

They also thought they would build a tower, so high that it would reach the sky. Then they would be famous all over the world.

God was sad about the people building a tower just to become famous. He also knew that they could only do this work because they all spoke the same language and could understand each other.

So, God made the people speak different languages and the building of the tower had to stop. In time, it became known as 'The Tower of Babel', 'babel' meaning a muddle of different languages. Then God sent the people to live in other lands on the Earth.

God had punished people for their ambition and sinful pride.

Abraham

One day, God appeared to a man called Abraham.
'Look at the sky,' God told him. 'Count the stars.
That will be the number of your children's children.'

God then told Abraham that he must leave his home and move with his relations and his wife, Sarah, to a country called Canaan. There, Abraham would start his family. But Abraham and Sarah had no children.

*S*arah had believed she could never have children. She had pleaded with Abraham to take her maid-servant, Hagar, as a wife, so that he might have a son. Both Hagar and Abraham knew that this was what Sarah wanted, so they agreed. One day, an angel appeared to Hagar. 'You must call your son Ishmael,' said the angel. 'Now you can return to Sarah.'

Three years after the birth of Ishmael, God appeared once more to Abraham. 'Sarah will have a son,' God told him. 'He will become the leader of a great people.' Abraham was surprised. Both he and Sarah were very old.

Three men sent by God told Abraham that his son's name would be Isaac. Abraham was a hundred years old when Isaac was born.

Some years later,
God told Abraham to
sacrifice his much-loved
son, Isaac. This was to
test Abraham's faith.
Obediently, Abraham built
a wooden altar and took a
knife. Just as he was about
to kill Isaac, he heard
God's voice.

God said, 'Stop, Abraham! Do not lay a hand on your son! I can see how much you love and obey your God. I shall bless you, your children and your children's children.' Then Abraham saw a ram with its horns caught in the bushes. He offered the ram to God instead of Isaac, his son.

47

The years passed. Abraham became older and his wife, Sarah, died. One day, Abraham called his most faithful servant to go into other lands to find a wife for his son, Isaac. He gave the servant money and camels for the long journey.

The servant prayed to God for a sign, so that he would know the right wife for Isaac. Just then, he saw a lovely young girl with a pitcher of water. She gave him water for himself and his camels. The servant thought that she must be the wife God had chosen.

The girl's name was Rebecca. Abraham's servant hurried to her house to explain to her parents who he was and why he was there. They all agreed that Rebecca could marry Isaac.

As Rebecca and the servant neared Abraham's home, a handsome young man came to meet them. Rebecca asked who this was. The servant said it was Isaac. They fell in love from that moment.

Joseph

and his Dreams

Isaac and Rebecca had two sons, Jacob and Esau. Jacob had twelve sons, but his favourite was Joseph. One day, Joseph told his brothers about a dream he had.
'We had been cutting corn,' he said, 'and all your sheaves bowed down to mine.'
His brothers did not like this.
'So do you think you are going to rule over us, like a king?' they asked.

Joseph's brothers all wanted to kill him, except the eldest, Reuben. Joseph had a coat of many colours that Jacob had given him. Reuben took the coat and smeared it with blood to make Jacob believe that Joseph had been killed by a wild animal. Reuben sold Joseph to merchants on their way to Egypt.

In Egypt, the merchants sold Joseph to Potiphar, Pharaoh's Captain of the Guard. At first, all was well. Then Potiphar's wife wanted Joseph to fall in love with her. Joseph would not. So she said that Joseph had attacked her and he was thrown into prison.

haraoh's cupbearer and baker were also in prison. 'I dreamed of a vine with three branches,' the cupbearer told Joseph. 'I picked grapes and pressed them into Pharaoh's cup and gave it to him.' Joseph said this meant the cupbearer would return to Pharaoh's court in three days. The baker had dreamed of carrying three baskets of bread on his head. The birds had pecked at the bread. Joseph said this meant that Pharaoh would kill the baker. Joseph was right.

59

*P*haraoh had also been having dreams. In one, he had seen seven fat cows feeding in a meadow, then seven thin cows ate the fat cows. In another, seven plump ears of corn had been destroyed by seven thin ears of corn. Nobody could understand these dreams. Then the cup-bearer told Pharaoh about Joseph. God gave the meaning of Pharaoh's dreams to Joseph.

*J*oseph said, 'Your dreams mean that your country will have seven years of plenty, then seven years of bad harvests. You need a wise man to store all the food and make sure there is enough for those years of bad harvests.' 'Nobody can be more wise than you,' said Pharaoh.

$\mathcal{E}$verything happened just as
Joseph said it would. One day, his brothers
came to Egypt to buy grain. Joseph recognized
them, but by now he was so rich and important
that they did not recognize him. He filled their
sacks with grain without asking for any money
and invited them for a meal.

*J*oseph told his servant to put a silver cup in the sack belonging to his youngest brother, Benjamin. Then he sent his guards after his brothers, accusing them of theft.

*J*oseph said, 'The man who stole the cup must stay here as my servant.' 'Take me, instead!' said Judah, another brother. 'My father will die if we go back without Benjamin!'

oseph knew then that his brothers were no longer
as cruel as they had been to him. 'I am your brother,
Joseph,' he told them. 'You and my father must all
come and live here, so that I can look after you.'

Then Joseph's servants gave his brothers everything that they needed for their long journey home.

So Jacob and his sons came to
Egypt. And after the bad times
were over, Joseph said that the
people need give only one fifth
of their harvest to Pharaoh.

This made the people very happy.
As well as serving Pharaoh,
they could now grow food
for themselves, too.

Moses

As the years passed, a new Pharaoh came to power. He feared that the Israelites would take over the country, because there were so many of them. So, he set them to work as slaves.

This Pharaoh also ordered every new-born Israelite boy to be killed. Baby girls would be spared, because they could become servants.

One Israelite woman had a son. To save him from being killed, she put him in a basket which she hid in the rushes by the river. Pharaoh's daughter was nearby. She heard the cries of the baby and found the basket. 'He shall be as my son,' she said. 'I shall call him Moses.'

$\mathcal{M}$oses grew
into a strong, young man.

When Moses saw an Israelite being ill-treated by an Egyptian, he killed the Egyptian and had to flee into the desert. In time, Moses became a shepherd. One day, he came across a bush which was on fire, yet not burning away. 'Moses,' came the voice of God. 'I have seen how cruel Pharaoh is to the Israelites. Return to Egypt and find Aaron your brother. Then go and tell Pharaoh to set my people free. I will help you.'

*M*oses did as God asked. He and Aaron pleaded with Pharaoh to set the Israelites free. But Pharaoh refused. Then Aaron showed the power of God. He picked up a stick and it became a snake.

*P*haraoh's magicians could also change sticks into snakes. But Aaron's snake ate up all the others.

*S*till Pharaoh would not let the Israelites go. So God turned the waters of the River Nile into blood. Frogs, then flies and insects infested the Egyptians. There was famine, an outbreak of boils and violent storms. Pharaoh had to allow Moses to lead the Israelites out of Egypt. Then came the final plague. On their last night in Egypt, the Israelites smeared blood on their doors. Then an angel came from heaven. He passed over the homes where the doors were smeared with blood. But at all other homes where the angel went, the eldest son died. This made everyone so scared, that the Pharaoh had to allow Moses to lead the Israelites out of Egypt.

Then Pharaoh changed his mind. He ordered his army to bring the Israelites back. The Israelites had come to a stop by the Red Sea, when they saw the Egyptians. As Moses reached out his stick towards the sea, God sent a wind to make a path through the waters so that they could cross. When the Egyptians tried to follow, the waters came together again and they were drowned.

Moses began leading the Israelites across the desert. They walked for many, many days and became very hungry.

God had told Moses that he would send food for his people. Next day, the ground was covered with white grains. 'It is the food that God promised us,' said Moses. They called the food manna.

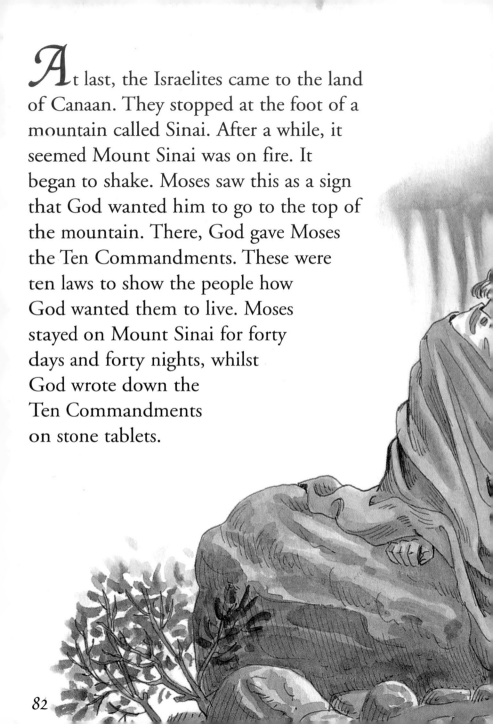

At last, the Israelites came to the land of Canaan. They stopped at the foot of a mountain called Sinai. After a while, it seemed Mount Sinai was on fire. It began to shake. Moses saw this as a sign that God wanted him to go to the top of the mountain. There, God gave Moses the Ten Commandments. These were ten laws to show the people how God wanted them to live. Moses stayed on Mount Sinai for forty days and forty nights, whilst God wrote down the Ten Commandments on stone tablets.

By the time Moses came down from the
mountain, the Israelites had built a golden calf to
worship. Moses was angry. In his rage, he broke the
stone tablets and melted down the golden calf.
But God made new stone tablets and once more the
Israelites agreed to follow Moses.

King *Solomon*

*S*olomon was the son of King David of Israel. One night, God appeared to Solomon in a dream and asked what he would most like to have. 'Wisdom to judge my people,' Solomon answered. God was pleased that Solomon had not asked for glory or riches.

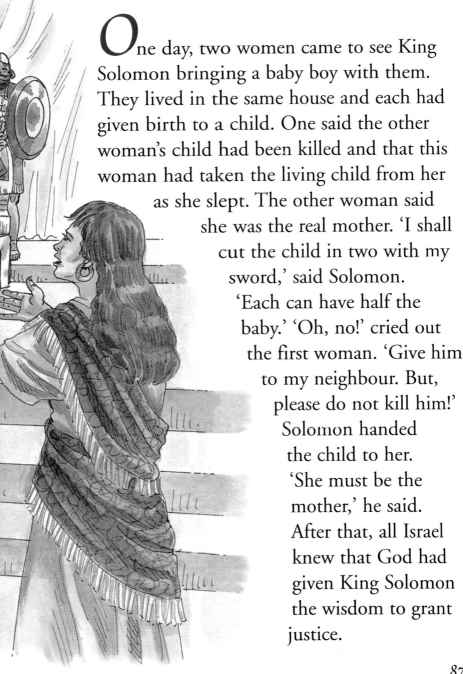

One day, two women came to see King Solomon bringing a baby boy with them. They lived in the same house and each had given birth to a child. One said the other woman's child had been killed and that this woman had taken the living child from her as she slept. The other woman said she was the real mother. 'I shall cut the child in two with my sword,' said Solomon. 'Each can have half the baby.' 'Oh, no!' cried out the first woman. 'Give him to my neighbour. But, please do not kill him!' Solomon handed the child to her. 'She must be the mother,' he said. After that, all Israel knew that God had given King Solomon the wisdom to grant justice.

$\mathcal{A}$s God had promised, the wisdom of Solomon lasted throughout his reign. People came from many lands to hear his wise words and to marvel at his intelligence.

$\mathcal{M}$any of his subjects came to Solomon for advice, knowing they would get justice from his wise and clever mind.

*I*n fact, the people of Israel loved their king so much that they began bringing him valuable gifts. Soon, the riches of Solomon were as famous as his wisdom. To show his thanks, Solomon began to build a great temple for God.

*T*he work took seven years. It was splendid. Walls were covered with gold, there were golden decorations and fine timbers of cedar wood.

*I*n time, the fame of Solomon came to the ears of the Queen of Sheba. She decided to visit him. She arrived in great splendour, bringing gifts for the king. 'Now,' she said, 'I see with my own eyes that you are even wiser and richer than people say. Blessed be Thy God.'

King Solomon married
many foreign women, and they
worshipped other gods.
Solomon also began worship-
ping these gods. This angered
God so much, he decided that
Solomon's son would not inherit
the kingdom. Instead, it would
be one of Solomon's ministers, a
man called Jeroboam.

Ahijah was a prophet sent by God. He tore his cloak in twelve pieces. 'Take ten pieces,' he told Jeroboam. 'God has said that the kingdom of Israel will be taken from Solomon. Then ten tribes will be given to you, as the new King.' This is what happened. Solomon's son, Rehoboam, ruled over just one tribe in Jerusalem.

When Solomon died, Rehoboam came to the throne. But the people of Israel did not like his harsh rule and cruel ways. They rebelled against Rehoboam and he had to flee to Jerusalem. Then the people made Jeroboam their king. But when Jeroboam also began building an altar with a golden calf, God was angry. As a sign of his great anger and power, God broke the altar and destroyed the golden calf.

*J*eroboam took no notice of this.
So God said that disaster would
come to him and his people.

*R*ehoboam and
Jeroboam went to war.
Jeroboam's people were killed
and their homes burned.

John the *Baptist*

In the reign of King Herod there lived a priest called Zacharias and his wife Elizabeth. They were old and had no children. One day, when Zacharias was at the temple, an angel appeared. 'You and Elizabeth will have a son,' said the angel. 'His name will be John. He will prepare the way for the coming of the Lord.'

 $\mathcal{E}$ lizabeth did not
know what to think at
first. But a few months
later, her cousin Mary
came to see her. Mary
told Elizabeth that she,
too, had been visited
by an angel and was
going to have a son.
He would be the
Son of God.

As soon as she heard Mary's words, Elizabeth felt her unborn baby kicking for joy. She was so happy to know that the angel's words would come true.

$\mathcal{A}$s for Zacharias - from the moment he had left the temple, he had been speechless. When a son was born to him and Elizabeth, all their friends were pleased. They wanted to know the child's name. 'His name is John,' Zacharias wrote on a tablet. Almost the same moment, he found he could speak once more.

Zacharias was filled with the Holy Spirit.
'Blessed be God!' he cried. 'His angel told me that my
son would prepare the way for the Son of God to
come and save the people!'

When John became a man, he preached the word of God on the banks of the River Jordan. 'God's King is coming!' he told people. 'Be sorry for your sins and you will be forgiven.'

$\mathcal{A}$ll the people who confessed their sins, were baptized by John in the River Jordan. He became known as John the Baptist.

Some priests asked John the Baptist, 'Are you the Christ? Are you the Saviour who has come to save Israel, as the prophets told us? Or, are you a prophet yourself?'

'I have only come to prepare the way of the Lord,' said John. 'I baptize with water, but the one who comes after me is mightier than I am. He will baptize with the Holy Spirit.'

John said that those who were baptized must lead good lives. 'What must we do?' they asked.

'A person with two coats must give one to someone with no coat,' said John. 'Anyone with food must give some to a person with none.'

109

*J*esus came to the River Jordan to be baptized.
'You come to me to be baptized?' John said to
Jesus. 'It ought to be you baptizing me.'
'This is as it should be,' said Jesus.

*A*nd as John baptized Jesus, the heavens opened up and the Holy Spirit came down in the form of a dove. They heard a voice which said, 'This is my own dearly loved son. I am most pleased with him.'

Time passed and John carried on with preaching and baptizing the people. But King Herod's wife hated him. She forced Herod to imprison John the Baptist and then made a plan so that he would lose his head. John's life and his work was over.

The Birth and Boyhood of *Jesus*

Mary lived in a little town called Nazareth. She was engaged to be married to Joseph. One day, the Angel Gabriel appeared. 'You will be visited by the Holy Spirit so that you will have a son,' Gabriel told Mary. 'His name will be Jesus, and he will be the Son of God.'

When Joseph learned that Mary was going to have a baby, he did not know what to do. Then he had a dream, where an angel spoke to him. 'Do not be afraid to take Mary as your wife,' the angel said. 'She is expecting a child through the power of the Holy Spirit. The child will be called Jesus and he will save the world from its sins.'

*T*he moment he awoke, Joseph remembered what the Angel of the Lord had said. He would marry Mary.

When the time
came for Mary's baby to
be born, she and Joseph had
to go to Bethlehem to be taxed.

Only a stable could be found. There, Mary gave birth to her son. Then, the Angel of the Lord gave the wonderful news to some shepherds. They came to see the baby and to praise God.

*T*hree wise men from the east had come to Jerusalem. 'Where is the baby who is born to be King of the Jews?' they asked Herod. 'We have followed his star from the east.'

*H*erod did not know. But he hated the idea of another king. The men followed the star until it stopped above the place where Jesus was.

*T*hey brought him presents
of gold, frankincense and myrrh.

Not long afterwards, an angel appeared again to Joseph in a dream. 'Take the baby and Mary and flee to Egypt as fast as you can,' said the Angel. 'Herod is searching for the child so that he can kill him.' And so, Joseph, Mary and Jesus fled to Egypt.

Meanwhile, Herod was determined to kill the child that the wise men had called King of the Jews. All baby boys under the age of two years were put to death on his orders.

*S*uch terrible killings brought great sadness to the whole country. But Herod greatly feared the power of someone who had been called King of the Jews.

Before they fled to Egypt, Joseph and Mary had brought Jesus to the temple when he was eight days old. Here, they presented the baby to God, according the law of Moses.

After Herod died, an Angel of the Lord appeared to Joseph in a dream to tell him that it was now safe to return to Israel. So, Joseph, Mary and Jesus all came back to live in Nazareth.

When Jesus was twelve years old, he went with Mary and Joseph to Jerusalem to celebrate the Feast of the Passover. When this was over, Jesus was not with them. They found him three days later in the temple, talking with the wise men there. 'Don't you know that I must be about my father's business?' he said. Jesus was talking about God, his father.

The Preaching of Jesus

*O*ne day, Jesus had been preaching from a fishing boat on Lake Gennesaret. When he had finished, he told Simon to lower the nets. Instantly, they were filled with fish. Yet no fish had been caught the whole night before. Those fishermen were his first disciples.

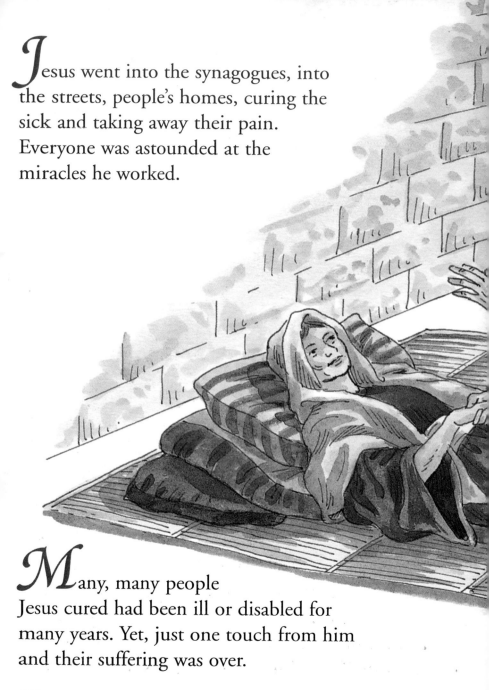

Jesus went into the synagogues, into the streets, people's homes, curing the sick and taking away their pain. Everyone was astounded at the miracles he worked.

Many, many people Jesus cured had been ill or disabled for many years. Yet, just one touch from him and their suffering was over.

*J*esus worked a miracle at a wedding in Cana. During the wedding feast, the family found they had no wine.

*J*esus asked the servants to fill some water-pots with water. When this was done, Jesus drew some water out - but now, instead of water, it had become thc fincst winc!

Jesus warned his disciples, 'I send you out as sheep among a pack of wolves, so you must be as wise as serpents and as harmless as doves. Because you are my followers, you will be brought before governors and kings. But do not worry what you will say. The Holy Spirit will speak for you.'

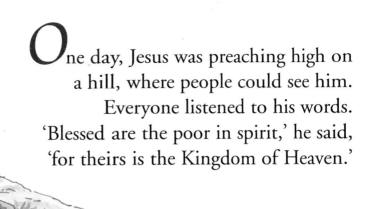

One day, Jesus was preaching high on a hill, where people could see him. Everyone listened to his words. 'Blessed are the poor in spirit,' he said, 'for theirs is the Kingdom of Heaven.'

Jesus taught his followers to love their enemies and to forgive those who did harm to them.

So many people began following Jesus, wanting to see him work miracles and to hear all he said. Once, a crowd of five thousand had stayed with him all day, without anything to eat.

A boy in the crowd gave Jesus five tiny barley loaves and two fishes. Jesus gave thanks to God. Then he told everyone to sit down in rows. He broke the loaves and fishes in pieces for his disciples to give to the people. All five thousand had more than enough to eat.

*A*t last, Jesus told his disciples to get in their boat and go out across the lake, whilst he sent the crowds on their way. Then, he went up into the mountain to pray. Night began to fall and Jesus did not return. All at once, there was a fierce storm. A strong wind blew across the sea. Through all this, the disciples saw Jesus walking on the water, as the boat was being tossed about by the waves. 'Truly,' said the disciples, 'you are the Son of God.'

*L*azarus, a friend of Jesus, was very ill. His sisters, Mary and Martha, went to ask Jesus to come and cure their brother. When Jesus arrived, Lazarus had been dead four days. 'Your brother will rise again,' said Jesus. 'I am the resurrection and the life. Whoever believes in me, even though he is dead, will live.'

*J*esus asked Martha to move the stone covering the tomb where Lazarus was buried. Then he called: 'Lazarus, come here!' At once, Lazarus came out of the tomb, alive once more. Everyone marvelled at such a miracle.

*J*esus cured many people of all kinds of suffering. One day, he met a man who had been born blind. Jesus mixed some earth with his own saliva and put the mud on the man's eyes. When the man washed it off, he could see.

Jesus *in Jerusalem*

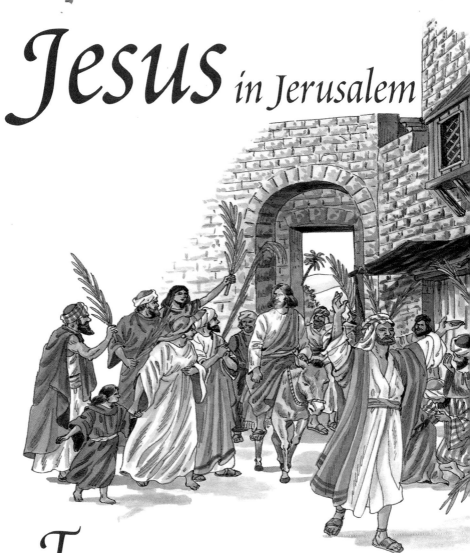

The Feast of the Passover was drawing near and Jesus came into Jerusalem on a donkey. 'Blessed is the King who comes in the name of God!' the people cried. Many laid down leaves from the palm tree.

146

As it was near the Feast of Passover, there were many people in Jerusalem. When Jesus came to the temple, he was angry to see money-changers and merchants setting up stalls and selling all kinds of goods. He overturned their tables and sent the men on their way.

When the scribes and the Pharisees heard about this, they were so angry. People took more notice of Jesus than them! They tried to trap him with a question. 'Master,' they said, 'you teach the ways of God. Tell us, is it right to give to Caesar, or not?'

Jesus asked, 'Whose image is on a coin?'
'Caesar's,' they answered.
'Then give to Caesar what is Caesar's,' said Jesus. 'And give to God what is God's.'

*J*esus knew that the scribes and the Pharisees were against him and that soon he would be put to death. So he went outside Jerusalem to have a Passover supper with his disciples for the last time.

*J*esus blessed the bread and gave it to his disciples. Then he blessed some wine and passed it around. 'Do this in remembrance of me,' he said.

After the Last Passover Supper, Jesus and his disciples went to pray in a garden on the Mount of Olives. Jesus walked a little way from the others. He fell on his knees and began to pray. 'Father,' said Jesus, 'please do not let me suffer, but only if this is what you want.'

As Jesus spoke, an angel came down to him from heaven to give him strength.

Soon afterwards, Jesus was seized by the guards of the high priests. He was taken to one of their houses.

Was he the Son of God, they asked? 'Yes,' Jesus answered, 'if you say that I am.' 'Blasphemy!' they shouted. 'He mocks God!' Some spat in the face of Jesus and poked fun at him.

Jesus was brought before the Roman Governor,
Pontius Pilate. He wanted to free Jesus.
'We can release a prisoner at Passover,' said Pilate.
'Shall it be Jesus? Or shall it be the thief, Barabbas?'
He was sure the people would not choose Barabbas.
'Release Barabbas!' they cried. 'Crucify Jesus!'
Pilate washed his hands to show he did not
want the blood of Jesus on them.

The Death and Resurrection of Jesus

*P*ontius Pilate had to do what the priests said.
He had to release the thief Barabbas.
The soldiers led Jesus away to be crucified.

The soldiers stripped Jesus of his clothes and put a crown of thorns on his head. Then they mocked him, laughed and spat at him and hit him with a cane.

Saint Paul
the Apostle

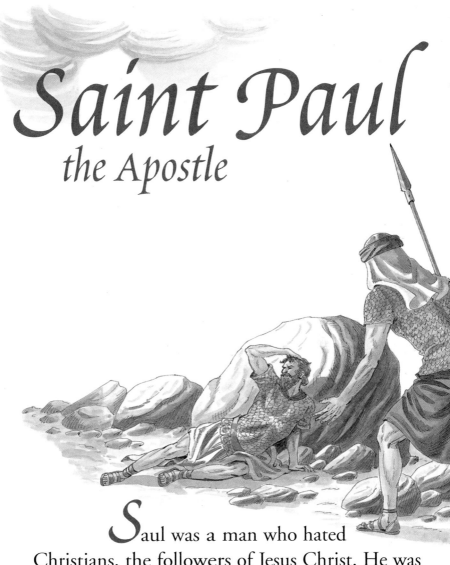

*S*aul was a man who hated
Christians, the followers of Jesus Christ. He was
cruel to them and put many in prison. One day on
the road to Damascus a light shone down, so strong
that it made him fall. 'Saul,' came the voice of Jesus.
'Why do you hate me so?'

*S*aul trembled.
'What must I do?' he
asked. 'Go into the
city,' came the reply.
When Saul got up,
he could not see.
People led him into
Damascus and Saul
found his way into
a house. Soon,
a man called
Ananias arrived.

*J*esus had appeared to Ananias and told him about Saul. Ananias had been surprised. Saul was well-known for his cruelty to Christians. 'Saul,' he said, 'the Lord Jesus sent me to restore your sight and so that you would be filled with the Holy Spirit.' The moment Ananias touched him, Saul could see. Soon after, he was baptized.

After that, Saul went about telling the people about Jesus. Because of this, the Jews in Damascus decided to kill him and he had to flee to Jerusalem. There, he came to know Barnabas, one of the disciples of Jesus. Together, they journeyed to Antioch (now in Turkey) and to Cyprus to spread the Christian faith. By this time, Saul had changed his name to Paul.

In some places,
Paul and Barnabas were hated
and they had to flee. But in others,
they were made welcome.

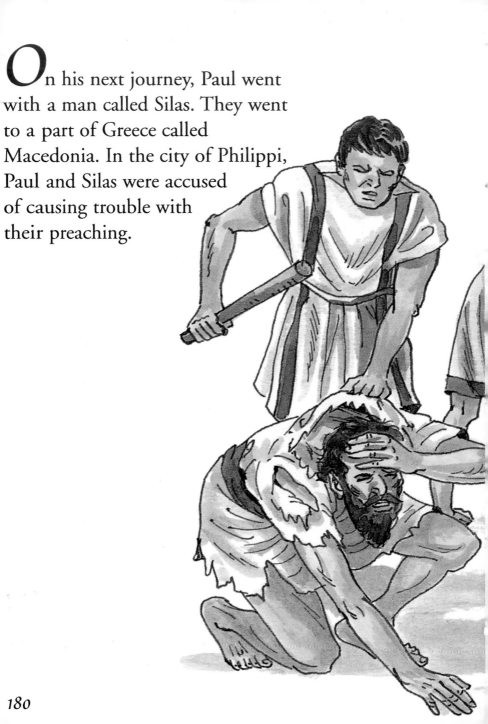

On his next journey, Paul went with a man called Silas. They went to a part of Greece called Macedonia. In the city of Philippi, Paul and Silas were accused of causing trouble with their preaching.

The city guards beat Paul
and Silas with sticks and
threw them in prison.

In Athens, Paul explained to the people that the statues of the gods in their city were false gods and that he, Silas and another man called Timothy, preached the word of the true God.

On their third journey, Paul and Timothy went to Ephesus (now in Turkey). There, they met people who had been baptized by John the Baptist, but who did not know about the power of the Holy Spirit.

Paul put his hands on the head of each of these people and baptized them in the name of Jesus.

*T*hrough the power of the Holy Spirit, they began speaking different languages.

For the rest of his life, Paul preached the word of Jesus everywhere he went on his long journeys. He wrote many letters to the Christian followers in the countries he visited, to help people live their lives as God wanted and to keep their Christian faith.